Building the Crosby Catboat

Crosby catboat replica *Breck Marshall. (Photo by Mary Anne Stets)*

Building the Crosby Catboat

by Barry Thomas

Mystic Seaport Museum, Inc.
Mystic, Connecticut • 1989

To Horace Manley Crosby, Jr.

"They have been building catboats on Cape Cod for the best part of a hundred years, and the Cape cat is the commonest boat to be seen between Plymouth and Point Judith."

Winfield Thompson
The Rudder, March 1909

Contents

Preface

The popularity of the catboat as a cruising boat today is in large part attributable to Breck Marshall. A longtime devotee and observer of this boat type, Breck Marshall designed and built fiberglass cats in several models and sizes, of which there are hundreds now in service. It was, therefore, fitting for the Catboat Association to approach Mystic Seaport Museum with the funds for building a catboat to be exhibited at the Museum as a memorial to Breck Marshall.

That boat was built in 1986-87, as is described in this book, and she is now sailed by the Museum on the Mystic River.

Fig. 1. Crosby boatshops at Osterville, ca. 1910. In the center of the picture is the shop of H. Manley Crosby. To the right of that are the shops of Wilton Crosby and Charles Crosby. The corner of Herbert Crosby's shop is visible on the right margin of the photo. (*Courtesy Horace Manley Crosby, Jr.*)

Introduction

Even excluding Native American craft, the differing kinds of traditional Northeastern American boats is far more in number than one would suppose; each town, village, and cove had its specialty. Interestingly, frustratingly, each of these had its own special way of being built, dozens of trade tricks, methods which evolved and were borrowed over generations. Most of this knowledge has dropped out of our culture—simply disappeared. One hardly realizes the extent of this loss until attempting to replicate these craft.

Fortunately, the Catboat Association's Breck Marshall Memorial Fund provided Mystic Seaport Museum's Boat Shop with the means to research and construct a working Cape Cod catboat. We chose a boat built by the Crosbys of Osterville, Massachusetts. This book is a summation of what we found and did.

Among the various stories about the origins of the catboat on Cape Cod, Howard Chapelle's is perhaps the most compelling: "the late H. Manley Crosby told me that his father, Horace S. Crosby (who built the first Crosby catboat with his brother Worthington in the 1850s), saw the first catboat he had ever seen in Narragansett Bay. He described the boat as being one of the centerboard class there." (quoted in John Leavens, *The Catboat Book* [Camden, Maine: International Marine, 1971])

This boat, with its particular shape and characteristics, was firmly established by the Crosbys. For three generations Crosbys were the best-known builders of the type, and from their shops came the majority of these boats. Usually there were several Crosby shops in business; around 1900 there were five, operated by Daniel, Horace Manley, Charles, Wilton, and Herbert (see fig. 1). But in all the shops the boats were built essentially the same way, according to Horace Manley Crosby, Jr. We, therefore, use the name Crosby collectively to refer to all of those shops.

It is the intent of this book to record what we found to be unique in the Crosby methods, which were in use from before 1880 through the building of the last catboat in the winter of 1934-35. After World War II, methods and materials changed, drastically. What is common boatbuilding practice, as described in books such as Howard Chapelle's *Boatbuilding* and Robert Steward's *Boatbuilding Manual,* has not been repeated here, except for purposes of continuity.

The boat was researched, measured, drawn, and built by the Mystic Seaport Museum Boat Shop: Bret Laurent, Clark Poston, and Barry Thomas, and volunteers Osdel Ostiguy and Chester Rice.

Our objective was to build a working, pre-engine (ca.1903) Crosby catboat. The last traditionally built Crosby catboat, *Sea Robin,* was launched over fifty years ago. As we began to look at the remaining boats, we found most to be extensively rebuilt, but the few with original work intact revealed the unexpected, what one of us, John Gardner, who knows perhaps more than any other, called "unique."

It is the purpose of this book to describe what those uniquenesses (for

Fig. 2. Horace Manley Crosby, Jr., upon his retirement from the Crosby boatyard, 1978. *(Courtesy Horace Manley Crosby, Jr.)*

there are a few) are and, where possible, how they were done. It is not always possible to infer the how from the what—that is, how something was done from what was done. Or, as Bret Laurent said, "old boats don't talk." No, they don't; not like old boatbuilders anyway.

Of course, we could have built a boat that in all respects looked like a Crosby catboat, using methods familiar to us. Why, indeed, should one attempt to do it their way? There is a very pressing answer. It is more than possible that these evolved methods, methods refined over the years, taken from who knows what other line of evolution, were more economical and logical in all ways—that is to say better—than methods that we now, more than fifty years after the last one was built, could possibly devise given the same materials and shape of boat. That is, I feel, a certainty, but it is one that hardly any amateur in his uncertainty, or any professional wooden builder who is unable to rise above his own past, or anyone fascinated by modern technology, can digest. Too bad. Consider the Stradivarius violin and the many failures to successfully reproduce this instrument and its sound. It would seem, in this sense, that old violins don't talk much either.

Luckily for us, there was a guide to lead us through the maze of hints and suggestions, a man who worked in his father's shop from 1924 through 1931. He then moved to another part of the business, retaining in his memory a snapshot, firmly remembered in parts, a bit hazy in others, of the methods of that time. This man is Horace Manley Crosby, Jr., or "Bunk" Crosby to those who know him (see fig. 2). To him we respectfully and gratefully dedicate this book.

Sources

For building the boat, our sources of information were boats, plans, *The Rudder* magazine, and a few boatbuilders.

The Boats

Trio: a 14-foot open Wilton Crosby catboat in the collection of Mystic Seaport Museum. Her construction is mostly original.

Sarah: a 19-foot Herbert Crosby catboat owned by John Church of Lenox, Massachusetts. Her cockpit and centerboard case had been removed, revealing a great deal of original construction that was of much interest to us.

Tryphaena: a 20-foot catboat said to be Crosby built, owned by Jean Crosby of Osterville, Massachusetts. She was extensively rebuilt; however, it was her hull that we measured for our reproduction. She is a very beautiful boat. Tradition, and the considerable deadrise of her transom, would seem to place her building date at 1900 or earlier.

Frances: a 21-foot Wilton Crosby catboat in the collection of Mystic Seaport Museum. Considering her construction changes, she was of little help to us except in matters of trim and finish.

Dover: A 27-1/2-foot Daniel Crosby catboat, owned by Robert Douglas of Vineyard Haven, Massachusetts. She is a virtually pristine boat, which we found after we had nearly finished our project. Wonderfully, she confirmed what we had done.

The Plans

The plans are owned by Crosby Yacht Yard, Inc. (formerly Crosby Yacht Building and Storage Company) to whom we are grateful for access to these plans. Of the drawings concerning catboats, only one shows construction details; the others, apart from sail plans, are "Keel and Setting Up Plans." Invariably these show the backbone of the boat (the stem, mast step, keel, deadwood, transom) and dimensions for the transom and usually two molds, one right forward and one right aft of the centerboard case. The majority of these drawings were done between 1902 and 1915 by Ralph Crosby, the son of Daniel.

The Rudder Magazine

In its March 1909 issue, *The Rudder* contains an article by Winfield Thompson entitled "*Sea Wolf,* Cruising Cat," which describes his 28-foot Daniel Crosby-built catboat. This article includes three photographs of the boat under construction.

The Boatbuilders

We had help from Brad Crosby, Wilton Crosby, Jr., and Richard Pierce, all of whom worked for Crosby Yacht Building and Storage, but later than our period of interest. Our main source was H. Manley Crosby, Jr. (Bunk Crosby).

He did not know or remember everything, but his contribution was enormous; without him, nothing. He was the missing link between what we saw as we studied the boats and the knowledge of how it was done. Bunk timbered out the boats, planked, decked, and finished them, but did not get out the keels, stems, or deck beams. These things were left for the older men. For example, note this from an interview John Leavens did with Captain Malcolm Crosby, 3-4 August 1963:

> J.L.   "In a standard catboat what is the distance from the stem to the center of the mast hole?   Is there a standard rule of thumb for that?"
>
> M.C.   "No. I don't think so. I can't tell. My father and Uncle Wilton, they always laid it out you know."

An interesting answer. Knowledge is power.

Fig. 3. Stem crook. *(Photo by Nancy d'Estang)*

Construction

Throughout this discussion, refer to the *Breck Marshall* construction drawings. Note that all the early Crosby catboats were fastened with iron, galvanized. Iron being no longer available, we used silicon bronze.

The Backbone

The backbone found in all the old boats we looked at is, in method, exactly as shown in the Ralph Crosby drawings (see plan 1 for his drawing of a 22-foot boat). It could not be more simple, and it possesses great strength.

The stem in the *Marshall* is sided five inches and molded about six inches. It must be got out of a white oak crook (see fig. 3), as were all Crosby catboat stems.

Do not suppose that these stems were not green or that unseasoned backbone stock is even undesirable. Well-seasoned and air-dried oak would swell far too much (3/4 inch in 12 inches) after the newly built boat was launched. It is not desirable that what was so carefully put together should swell 3/4 of an inch (sometimes different pieces in different directions) when put in use. It would perhaps be desirable to season oak timbers in salt water before using, but this is a luxury that takes years. It is of interest to note that the *Marshall's* rudder, which is planked longitudinally, swelled 3/4 of an inch, causing the tiller to bind on the upper edge of its slot in the coaming and the two upper pintles to lift off their gudgeons. It is even more interesting to note

Fig. 4. Daniel Crosby, with the mast step and stem of *Sea Wolf.* (*The Rudder, March 1909*)

Fig. 5. Shaping the keel. *(Photo by Claire White-Peterson)*

that most of this swelling did not occur during her first five months in the water (cold winter months), but, rather, in the spring when the river warmed up.

The stem-to-keel connection is made by the white oak mast step (see fig. 4). It is sided six inches and in our boat is seven inches deep with a bit of curve in the grain forward to give room for fastenings into the stem. The Crosbys used galvanized iron drifts; we, however, used half-inch bronze bolts. The mast and 400 square feet of sail punch down here, up in her eyes, and it is the mast step and its fastenings to the keel and stem, and also the planking, that resist this pressure.

The keel is white oak, 7-1/2 inches sided; it is brought to its molded shape by adze (see fig. 5). The top of the keel is usually a straight line—or three straight lines: a straight line from the forward end down to the centerboard slot; then, at a slight angle to the first, a straight line the length of the slot; and then another straight line from there aft. In the Ralph Crosby drawings, the top of the keel in the way of the slot is slightly raised, the keel fore and aft of it being lower, presumably to allow room enough for some depth to the cabin floor and floor timbers, and at the same time to give more strength in the way of the centerboard slot. (Twenty-five or so years ago Howard Davis and Arnold Crossman of Noank, Connecticut, put a new keel in a Crosby catboat. The old keel was several inches higher in the way of the centerboard case than the rest of the keel. We talked to no one else who remembers this type of keel.)

For the *Breck Marshall*, the centerboard slot was cut by handsaw, starting it with auger holes and finishing it with a slick. As an alternative, the Crosbys sometimes kerfed the keels in the way of the slot, making a single saw cut, which was wedged open at either end. After the "standards" (head ledges) were fitted, the keel was drifted athwartships to prevent further splitting. Thus, a keel with a sawn and wedged slot can be got out of timber narrower than that for a keel with a sawn and cut out slot.

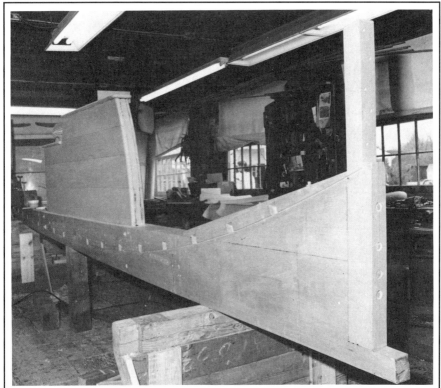

Fig. 6. The deadwood and stern post. Note the centerboard trunk in place. *(Photo by Claire White-Peterson)*

The deadwood is stacked on the keel aft as much as is needed to allow for the rise of the rabbet to the transom and to give enough wood to allow for the timber holes (see figs. 6 and 7). This, however, is not necessary where floor timbers can tie the timbers (frames) to the keel, and often the timbers were simply bird-beaked on top of the keel (notched at the end to fit over the upper corners of the keel). The keel may be notched here to allow the bird-beaked timbers to come down to the rabbet (see fig. 8).

Timber Holes

The half-dovetailing of the timbers into the keel was probably a Crosby invention; others such as Manuel Swartz of Edgartown also used it (see *Breck Marshall* construction drawings and plan 1). The hole or mortise into the keel is l-3/4 inches square (the size of the timber). Inside, the mortise is widened to form a female half-dovetail. The timber with its end half-dovetailed is fitted into the hole and then pushed fore or aft, as the case may be, so that the dovetail joint closes and a wedge is firmly tapped into the space left alongside the timber, thus holding the joint firmly in place. A boat nail was drilled for and driven up through the timber into the keel, this being added insurance.

The timber holes go $1\frac{1}{4}$ inches into the keel; their depth into the keel

Fig. 7. The transom and deadwood of *Sea Wolf* set up in Daniel Crosby's shop. *(The Rudder, March 1909)*

Fig. 8. In the catboat *Sarah*, the after timbers are bird-beaked on top of the deadwood. A floor would be fitted to tie these timbers to the keel. *(Photo by Peter Vermilya)*

Fig 9. Timber holes bored for (four holes for each timber hole). Note the centerboard trunk. *(Photo by Mary Anne Stets)*

Fig. 10. In the catboat *Sarah,* the top of the keel is grooved to receive the tongue of the bottom board of the tongue-and-groove centerboard case. *(Photo by Peter Vermilya)*

Fig. 11. Building the *Breck Marshall's* centerboard case. *(Photo by Mary Anne Stets)*

alongside the case adds to the width of the keel needed here. Sometimes there was trouble with leaking if the screw of the auger used to start these holes penetrated the inside of the centerboard slot. We used a Forstner bit to start a hole (see fig. 9) and finished it with a chisel. This was done at the beginning, while the keel could still be turned either side up on horses. An angle must be cut on the top of the timber hole: this is the angle at which the timber enters the hole, the angle of deadrise. This angle may be obtained from the lofting or half model.

A feature of the centerboard case construction deserves notice: the joint between the case boards is tongue-and-groove, and this includes the joint between the keel and the first board (see fig. 10). After the centerboard slot is cut in the keel, the case is built up from the keel (see fig. 11).

The Setup

As can be seen from the photograph of Daniel Crosby's shop (fig. 12), the keel of the boat is simply blocked up from the floor forward. Although Bunk Crosby told us that his father said "you can't have too many molds," Daniel Crosby did with very few. According to Ralph Crosby's drawings (see plan 1), boats up to 25 feet have generally two molds, one right fore and one aft of the centerboard case. A 35-foot "Cat Cruising Launch" had only three molds. This reserve is corroborated by figure 12, which shows only three molds used by Daniel Crosby for Winfield Thompson's 28-foot *Sea Wolf.* A drawing for a 17-foot, 3-inch catboat shows a third mold forward, a couple of feet abaft the stem. This is necessary, as we found, to get the hollow in the bow if the boat's shape requires it.

The Ralph Crosby drawings show measurements for each mold and the transom. There are no fairing lines; that is, waterlines, buttocks, and diagonals. The shape of the molds and transom were no doubt taken from the half model. It is possible that the boats were not lofted and the molds and transom were got out directly from the measurements on the drawings. Bevels, such as those for the transom and stem rabbet, could be taken from the model.

The drawing for the 35-foot launch shows ribbands of 1 $\frac{1}{8}$ by 1 $\frac{1}{2}$ inch spruce spaced about a foot apart; however, the actual spacing was no doubt in the hands of the man in the shop. Given the mold spacing and the size of the ribbands, it is obvious that the timbers were not bent inside (or outside) this framework. Given the number of molds, it is also apparent that the shape of the boats is somewhat limited; for, as anyone who has drawn up a set of lines using

Fig. 12. Sea Wolf set up with molds and ribbands in Daniel Crosby's shop. *(The Rudder, March 1909)*

Fig. 13. *Breck Marshall* set up with two molds on the backbone. *(Photo by Mary Anne Stets)*

ducks and splines knows, some curves require more than two ducks to bend the batten through the curve. More properly, it should be said that considering the usual shape of a Crosby catboat, only two molds were needed to obtain that shape. The shape of our boat required, we found as we added them one by one, five molds. Figure 13 shows her with just two molds up.

Timbering Out the Boat

The Dilemma

If we can agree with Winfield Thompson that "the Cape cat is the commonest boat to be seen between Plymouth and Point Judith" and that interest in the catboat is still very strong, it is then very curious that knowledge of how they were built (indeed, by the most famous builders) was in large part not to be found in 1986, not readily at any rate.

The most important questions had to do with timbering out the boat. The timbers are 1-3/4 inches square and the turn of the bilge aft is very tight. Advice was various: make the timbers smaller (they need not be so large); kerf them; bend the timbers on the outside of the ribbands; beef up the setup; and so on. The fact, however, remained: the timbers were indeed 1-3/4 inches square, they were not kerfed, and the setup was no more than that shown in the photograph of Daniel Crosby's shop (fig. 12).

Then, seemingly to complicate matters, we found that in all of the Crosby cats we studied, the timbers canted towards the widest part of the boat; that is, the forward timbers raked aft to the widest part of the boat, becoming more plumb as they approached that point, and the after timbers raked forward, becoming more plumb until the widest part is reached where (as it turned out in the *Marshall*) there is one plumb timber. Why was this? No one knew.

Additionally, we had a clue from Winfield Thompson's 1909 *Rudder* article: "timbers, also of oak, are two inches square, steam-bent on forms, and put into place cold." So from this we began.

The First Try

Taking the lead from Winfield Thompson, we built several forms, getting their shape from the body-plan sections on our lofting and also putting some extra curve in the forms to overbend the timbers, allowing for their tendency to spring back. First we bent the timbers for the midship area of the boat. The next day we put them in the boat. Disappointingly, they did not quite fit the curve of the bilge. Was there too much spring-back? We tried again with the same results. One thing was apparent, however: since the timbers were put in cold, not much twist could be put in them and this caused them to cant towards the beamiest part of the boat. That was an answer to one question. It also meant that the timbers, raking as they do, need to have slightly less bend in them than an upright timber would require (small things can mean a lot).

Our goal was to build the boat as she would have been built before 1935 when the last Crosby catboat was built by the old generation of builders. We had

Fig. 14. Setting the timber mold to the curve of the hull. Note that the timber mold is set square to the ribbands and thus rakes towards midships. *(Photo by Mary Anne Stets)*

Fig. 15. Drawing the curve of the timber on the bending platform. *(Photo by Mary Anne Stets)*

one more chance at this. In truth it did not seem like much of one. We had been told that there was another Crosby in Osterville, but that early on he had gone into the office, where he stayed. We had not been encouraged to see him. Nevertheless, we called Horace Manley Crosby, Jr., or "Bunk" Crosby as he is more generally known. "Yes," he said, "I must have opened that steambox a thousand times when timbering out boats." We went down to Osterville in a hurry.

The Second Try - The Crosby Method

Bunk Crosby was our guide through timbering, planking, and decking the boat and in numerous other details. Bunk told us how and why to use the "timber mold" (see fig. 14). Previously, Townie Hornor and Richard Pierce had brought one by the shop and we had made a copy of it. The timber mold is a sort of chain made of wooden links bolted together so that it can assume different curves. Bunk told us how to make the bending form, bend the timber, stay it with a lath, and put it in the boat. This method is simple, fast, and works perfectly.

We begin by placing the timber mold inside the ribbands, putting one end into the timber hole, and keeping the timber mold pretty much square on the ribbands, which means it tips a little bit towards midships, as will the timber itself (see fig. 14). When the mold conforms to the shape of the boat (i.e., the inside of the ribbands) where we want to put the timber, we tighten the timber mold bolts so that it holds the curve and take it out of the boat. We then lay it on the bending platform (some heavy 3-inch planks roughly four by eight feet).

Using the timber mold as a guide, we draw the curve of the timber on the bending platform, giving it some over-bend to allow for spring-back (see fig. 15). A batten of some kind (we used an old bandsaw blade) is used to draw the fair curve. Around this curve, on its line, we nail oak blocking 4 to 5 inches wide and 1-3/4 inches thick; no thicker, that is, than the timbers (to which we must fasten stay laths). Our blocking was not continuous (as it should have been) so we put a steel strap around the blocks to prevent each timber from knuckling as it was bent.

One curve can serve for up to four pairs of timbers. The pairs other than the one whose shape is taken off the boat with the timber mold are placed next to the original timber on the side where the curve of the boat becomes greater (because it is relatively easy to open up the curve of a bent timber and nearly impossible to put more curve into one). Thus, for a boat with eighteen pairs of steam-bent timbers, we needed to use only five different curves.

When a timber comes out of the steambox, a "timber band" is fastened to it. The timber band is simply a steel strap with a right angle bent on one end so that it can hook over the end of the hot timber; there is a hole in the bent-over end of the strap through which a nail is driven to hold the strap in place. The other end of the strap is "jacked" (clamped) to the timber's lower end. The timber is bent around the form, jacking it to the blocking as is necessary (see fig. 16). Through a hole in the lower end of the timber band a nail is driven to fasten that end of the band, and the jack temporarily used for that purpose can be removed. The Crosbys had a special "timber jack," which had an eye on the end of the screw for attaching a purchase for bending larger timbers (one is in the possession of the Osterville Historical Society).

Fig. 16. Bending the timber. *(Photo by Mary Anne Stets)*

A stay lath is then nailed to the timber. The timber may now be removed from the form (see fig. 17) and another timber bent.

The next day the timbers are put in the boat. Bunk said that the half-dovetails were cut in the timbers before they were steam-bent. This is done on the Crosby-built Wianno Seniors as the timbers are bent directly on the outside of the ribbands; we, however, had difficulty with this for the distance from the dovetail to the curve of the bilge is critical. Our solution was to cut the dovetail after bending. To do this we put the timber mold in the boat and set it up again to the proper curve with its end well into the timber hole in the keel. We then laid the timber mold on the stay-lathed timber, locating it on the curve of the bilge and marking the length to the timber hole on the timber itself (see fig. 18). Then we cut the dovetail (see fig. 19) and got the length from there to the turn of the bilge dead right each time.

The dovetailed timber is then fitted to its timber hole. This done, it is put in the hole and wedged tight (see fig. 20). Later a screw is put through the timber up into the keel. Only now should the stay lath be released. We released the lath at the lower end so that, while still attached to the upper end of the timber, it could be used as a lever to put as much twist as possible into the timber (not much) as we jacked it to the ribbands. The timbers come very nicely to the ribbands and the jacks to hold them there go on from the keel up (see fig. 21). It is possible to timber out a boat in two days in this manner.

Fig. 17. With a cross spall attached, the bent timber is removed from the form. *(Photo by Mary Anne Stets)*

Fig. 18. Marking the dovetail end of the timber. *(Photo by Mary Anne Stets)*

Fig. 19. Cutting the timber dovetail. *(Photo by Mary Anne Stets)*

Fig. 20. Wedging the timber tight in the timber hole. *(Photo by Mary Anne Stets)*

Figure 22 is a composite photograph of the boat in frame (there is considerable length distortion in this composite), which shows clearly the raking of the timbers. How much or little a timber rakes depends in some degree on the oak itself, and variations from one boat to the next, or from one side to the other, are of no consequence. The "Backbone and Timber" drawing of the *Breck Marshall* (plan 3) is not meant to specify how much the timbers must rake, but only to indicate that there must be rake to the timbers.

Fig. 21. Jacking the timbers to the ribbands. *(Photo by Mary Anne Stets)*

Fig. 22. A composite photo of the *Breck Marshall* in frame, showing the midships rake of the timbers fore and aft. *(Photo by Mary Anne Stets)*

Fig. 23. Breck Marshall timbered out. (Photo by Mary Anne Stets)

The boats were timbered out from midships aft and then from midships forward. The two or three forwardmost timbers in a catboat are rather straight and are sawn out to shape. At first they should be a little heavy so that you can "work 'em off"; that is, bevel them. Remember that the ceiling ends on the first timber forward, so the inboard surfaces of these sawn timbers must be made fair with those of the timbers that are steam bent.

The wedges in the timber holes are cut flush with the keel, and in Bunk's time (but not in the older boats we saw) escutcheon pins were driven through the wedges into the keel. We did not do this, however.

At this point in the boat's construction John Gardner looked at the boat in frame with her timbers canting towards midships and said, "now, that is unique" (see fig.23).

Floor Timbers

Bunk Crosby never had the job of putting in floor timbers, but he cautioned us to be careful that the floor-to-timber fastenings were not put where they would interfere with the plank fastenings. The floors were drifted to the keel. Following the advice of Bunk's father ("You can't have too many floors") and Ralph Crosby's drawings, we put floor timbers wherever they could go. There can be no floors alongside the centerboard case, nor under the cabin floor where there is no room for any throat or depth to a floor timber. Consequently, there may be only one to three floors between the aft end of the mast step and the centerboard case.

Planking

It is, I believe, essential to use cypress for the planking. Given the Crosby construction, no matter what the original reasons for using cypress, the strength of cypress is essential. White cedar does not have it; although cedar might be used in a smaller, say 14-foot, boat. Certainly mahogany would be a very poor substitute, as it is not as rot resistant as cypress, and with its lack of compressibility it is a consistent frame-breaker. Cypress's drawbacks are impressive splinters and a tendency to develop shakes or checks. Yet, it steam bends very well, it also comes in the epic widths used in planking these cats, and it comes clear.

The Crosby planking method seems to be unique. As is practical, considering the shape of the catboat hull, the planking can range from 14 inches wide for the broad strakes to 1 inch wide at the turn of the bilge on the transom. The planks are not backed out to fit the curve of the hull; rather the timbers themselves are dubbed flat for each strake of planking as would be done for larger sawn-frame vessels. And then there is also the matter of "turning her down."

When we took the lines off *Tryphaena*, we took her planking lines as well and later transferred these to our molds, stem, and transom. After nailing bat-

Fig. 24. Timbers dubbed flat for strakes of planking. *(Photo by Mary Anne Stets)*

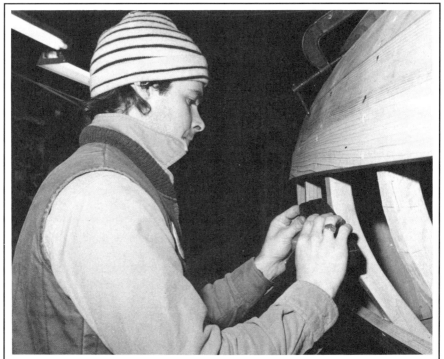

Fig. 25. Planing the timbers flat on the bilge. *(Photo by Mary Anne Stets)*

tens to these marks, we adjusted the battens to get the plank lines fair and then marked the plank lines onto the timbers. Lining off the planking was another job reserved for the older men; Bunk, however, remembered that a sheer batten was faired by eye and nailed to the timbers, the sheer being the lower edge of the batten. This faired sheer was leveled over to the other side of the boat with a carpenter's level and a straightedge.

Now with a fair run of planking marked on the timbers, the sheer planks and two or three planks below it are got out and hung on the boat. For each plank, the timbers are dubbed or planed flat between the mark on the timber for the upper edge of the plank and the mark for the lower edge (see figs. 24 and 25). Thus, the plank is not backed out except for several inches where planks land on the transom. Considering the thickness of the timbers, this method is quite practical, and it is very fast as well.

For spiling planks a "rule staff" was used. The rule staff is a fir or hardwood batten 1/4 inch thick and 3-1/2 to 4 inches wide. It should be as long as the longest piece of planking stock—16 feet in our case. Spiling the sheer strake, for example, the rule staff is bent to the hull, always without edgeset, and tacked to the timbers just below the sheer batten. Every three feet or so the distance between the sheer batten and the top edge of the rule staff is measured and this is marked on the rule staff. This is done in chalk so that it is easily cleaned off. In our shop we found this method difficult to apply, and we resorted to what we were familiar with: a spiling batten, made of enough pieces to put it close to the curving edge being spiled, and a compass for spiling. With planking stock no longer than 16 feet, each of our strakes had a butt. The rule for spacing butts is simply that two timbers must intervene between the butt on one strake and the next one above or below. The forward planks are called "forwards," the after ones, "afters." The "forwards" are always hung first. The "after" is then got out and clamped in place and a saw cut is run between the two ends at the butt to ensure a tight fit. A rap on the aft end of the "after" brings the butt ends tight together. The butt block is got out of timber stock. It is painted on the side that lies against the planking.

The butt blocks do not fit tight in between the timbers; rather, there is a 3/8- to 1/2-inch clearance between a block and timbers on either side. Early catboats had no butt blocks—their butts landed on the timbers; this is true of the Herbert Crosby catboat *Sarah*. The butting of planks on timbers makes repairs difficult, but *Sarah*'s butts are not failing any more quickly than the rest of the boat.

After the top three or four planks are hung on both sides and all her floor timbers are fastened in place, it is time to plank her up from the keel. To do this it is convenient to "turn her down." Looking at the photograph of Daniel Crosby's shop (fig. 12) we can see that the setup for Winfield Thompson's cat-boat is minimal—some blocking under the keel—and it could be that the after end of the keel rests on the shop floor. We had our boat blocked up a foot and a half or so, but this is no great matter. With the transom, stem, and molds freed from their restraints and supports, the boat is lowered down to the shop floor and turned down on one side. She is eased onto a 2-by-6-inch plank, six to eight feet long, which is blocked up at either end. Turned down on her starboard side, she presents a port side easily accessible for cleaning up the rabbet and for

Fig. 26. Breck Marshall turned down ready for her garboards. (Photo by Mary Anne Stets)

Fig. 27. With the hull turned down, the garboard is hung. *(Photo by Mary Anne Stets)*

planking. She is turned from side to side as planking proceeds, and it can be easily done by two people (see figs. 26, 27, and 28).

Figure 27 shows the rectangular Crosby limber. It gives as much area for its height (its height is how much it weakens the timber) as is possible. The desire to round the corners of the limber for fear of splitting in the corners is a misplaced concern for quality. The plank-to-timber fastenings on either side of the limber will prevent any splitting here.

There is nothing unique about the plank bevels. The edge that will lie against the plank already on the boat has its bevel taken from the edge of the plank on the boat and a timber. The timber being flat where the next plank will go makes this a very easy angle to take. Of course several bevels are taken along the length of the plank. The other edge of the plank is left square. A few shavings taken off both plank edges in the customary way provide a caulking seam. This should be about 1/16 of an inch on the outside.

On the broad strakes there are planks that require up to four fastenings per timber. On the *Marshall* there was always room for two fastenings on even the narrowest planks. The fastenings must be set deep enough to allow for smoothing off the hull, but apart from that, only enough setting of the fastening to allow for putty over the fastening head should be allowed—any more merely weakens the hull fabric.

When it is time to get out the next-to-last plank and the "fill-in" (shutter plank), the rule staff is tacked in place and measurements are made to the lower

Fig. 28. Planking up to the bilge. *(Photo by Mary Anne Stets)*

Fig. 29. Hanging the fill-in plank at the bilge. *(Photo by Mary Anne Stets)*

edge of the upper plank (these are for the fill-in) and to the upper edge of the lower plank (these are for the next-to-last plank.) These measurements are chalked on the rule staff and so is the total width between the two planks on the boat. Thus, this one marking of the rule staff gives us the upper edge of the fill-in plank and the lower edge of the next-to-last plank to be hung. The top edge of the next-to-last plank is obtained by dividing the total width to be filled by half, then laying a batten fairly through these width measurements on the planking stock. After this plank is hung and the top edge of the fill-in is marked on its planking stock, the widths of the shutter can be most accurately taken off the boat with a pair of dividers. Figure 29 shows the fill-in going on the boat.

As needed (which is often), "planking sets" or ordinary planking dogs are used with a wedge against the plank to set it tight against its neighbor. Do not expect too much when setting a 10-inch plank.

The Clamp

At this point, with the boat planked up, the molds should be removed, leaving a cross spall athwart the boat amidships (see fig. 30). The timberheads should be cut off flush with the sheer and pitched down towards the inside of the boat. As Bunk said, this makes fairing the deck beams and sheer much easier.

The clamp mercifully and logically has the shape of the tree: wide at the bow (bottom), tapering towards the stern (top). It is wider where the strength is most needed and where the hull shape is flatter, and it tapers as it goes aft and the bilge develops its tighter turn. It is, of course, necessary to plane off the outboard side of the clamp so that it will fit the curve of the boat. The clamp must be spiled. As seen in figure 30, we had to butt ours.

Note that the clamp is fastened to the first timber forward and is cut off there, not being in any way fastened to the mast partner. Back aft the clamp is cut off at the quarter knee and not fastened to that either (see fig. 31). It may seem like heresy, but the clamp does not tie the extreme ends of the boat to-

Fig. 30. On either side of the boat, the tapered clamp was put in in two pieces. *(Photo by Mary Anne Stets)*

Fig. 31. The main deck frame is let into the clamp on either side. *(Photo by Mary Anne Stets)*

gether; that is, the stem to the transom. There is no evidence that boats failed in any way because of this.

When the clamp was hung, the Crosby boatbuilders let its upper edge stand about a half inch above the sheer. This was to allow ample stock for the deck crown and for fairing in the deck and the sheer. Once the deck framing was in place, the upper edge of the clamp was taken down with a "big slice" and planed using the deck beams as a guide.

The Main Deck Frame

The main deck frame (beam) is flush to, and forward of, the cabin-cockpit bulkhead. This frame must go in now. It has a crown of 4-1/2 inches in ten feet. The location of our main deck frame necessitated a fore-and-aft piece fastened between two timbers for the forwardmost cockpit floor beam to land on (see the Profile and Half-Breadth Views of the *Breck Marshall*, plan 4). When the Herbert Crosby yard built *Sarah*, they positioned the main deck frame so that the first cockpit floor beam landed directly on a pair of timbers. Note that the deck frames have no direct connection to the timbers.

Letting Deck Frames Into The Clamp

Deck frames are let into the clamp and their ends are cut and beveled so that they are flush with the inside of the sheer plank. A fastening from the sheer plank into the end of each deck frame holds the frame in place. Later, the oak gunwale securely boxes in the outboard ends of the deck frames.

To begin, the deck frame is placed on the clamp and horned in (triangulated) to square it to the boat's centerline. With the frame as a guide, a line is struck on the top of the clamp. Using a rule against the sides of the frame, a line is struck down the side of the clamp for the forward side of the frame and again for the after side of the frame. Note that these lines are square to the sheer (not necessarily plumb.) Cut down these lines with a saw to within about 1/4 inch of the depth of the frame. Split out the wood between the cuts and then finish the

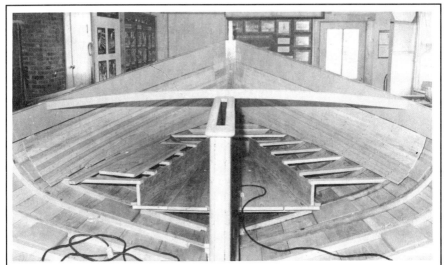

Fig. 32. In the cabin, the floor is laid, the transoms are framed on either side, and the ceiling is in. *(Photo by Mary Anne Stets)*

Fig. 33. The cabin ceiling and transom framing. *(Photo by Mary Anne Stets)*

Fig. 34. This view from the cockpit shows the cabin bulkhead staving on the after side of the main beam. *(Photo by Mary Anne Stets)*

notch until the deck frame lays about 1/16 to 1/8 inch below the inside edge of the sheer plank. All deck frames are let in thus.

Cabin Interior

It is now time to build the cabin interior: the cabin floor, transoms (seats), and ceiling (see fig. 32). This is straightforward work. Note that after leaving a slight gap for ventilation below the clamp, the ceiling is laid right down to the top of the transom framing (see fig. 33). The ceiling is made from resawn planking stock and finishes at 5/16 inch. Bead the stock first, before it is resawn: four pieces of beaded ceiling can be neatly cut from one piece of 7/8 inch by 3-1/8 inch cypress, allowing 1/8 inch for kerfs.

Cabin-Cockpit Bulkhead

This bulkhead is fastened to the main deck frame and the nailing cleats on the cabin floor and transom tops—note that the floor and transoms run aft of the bulkhead; they must go in first. The bulkhead is constructed of the same tongue-and-groove stock, chamfered on one side and beaded on the other, as the cockpit and forward bulkhead. Install the staving from the center out to the clamp and ceiling on either side. Let the staving be longer than need be for the cabin top; that should be cut down later.

The width of the side deck must be a multiple of deck planks plus the gunwale; don't cut into the bulkhead staving for the deck until after the gunwale is in and a few deck planks have been laid. This will make the cut more of a certainty (see fig. 34).

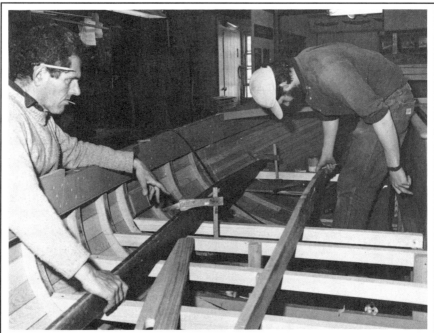

Fig. 35. Framing the cockpit floor. *(Photo by Mary Anne Stets)*

Cockpit Floor Beams

The framing for the cockpit floor is cypress or spruce. Each beam lands on top of a pair of timbers and may be notched over them.

First the aftermost beam and the forwardmost whole beam (the one just aft of the centerboard case) must be put in. Of course the forward pitch of the self-draining deck must be correct (putting her scuppers above the waterline!). Six inches is not too much pitch. Now lay two straightedges fore and aft on these two beams to get the intervening beam heights at the outboard ends. This is done by laying another straightedge athwart and beneath the fore-and-aft two and using the former to mark the heights of the beams on the timbers.

The camber is first put into the aftermost and forwardmost whole beams. After their ends are fastened to the timbers, camber is obtained in the floor beams by "jacking them right up" 1/2 inch or more. We did this with a block and two wedges between the top of the keel and the underside of the beam. Then two posts were fitted onto the floor on either side of the boat's centerline and finally one in the middle. These posts may have to be notched out to line up between the beam and floors. Now lay a straightedge down the center of the beams and jack up the intervening ones until they reach the straightedge height, then insert the posts under them.

The main thing to keep in mind is that the posts for the beams land on the floors. As the floors are not plumb, the beams must be placed so that their outboard ends get a good landing on the timbers, and at the same time the posts can brace them up from the floors.

The heights for the half-beams that fetch up against the centerboard case are established in much the same way (see fig. 35). However, they are not posted and their inboard ends land on a nailing piece fastened to the centerboard box. The forwardmost floor beam is nailed to the cockpit staving as well. Yes, these half-beams are straight, while the full ones have a camber posted in them, but it all works itself out as the deck is nailed down.

Cockpit Scuppers

There was a lot of advice, sought and unsought, concerning the scuppers; e.g., make them of flexible hose, not lead; screw them in place, for tacks are not secure enough; tack them at the very least, and so on. In the end we did none of those things. Bunk Crosby and Dick Pierce set us straight, and we did it in the old way, which proved to be the simplest way of all.

The scupper location should be as far forward in the cockpit and as far to the outboard edge as is possible. Of course, there are a few things inevitably in the way of putting them exactly where they should go: a plank seam in the hull, timbers, butt blocks, etc.

The scuppers were made from $1\frac{1}{2}$ inch lead pipe. The pipe was cut approximately to length with a couple of inches to spare. A piece of oak was turned to the inside diameter of the pipe and one end was rounded over to a bullet-like shape. This piece of oak was then driven through the section of pipe to straighten and make it round, for the lead will always be punched and bent out of shape a bit.

Where the scupper goes through the hull, drill a recess or rabbet two inches in diameter and 1/4 inch deep. Then, through the center of the rabbet drill a $1\frac{1}{2}$ inch hole square to the plank and through it. Round over the edge a bit so that the lead will not break there when it is bent over to form a lip. Do the same thing to the cockpit floor decking.

Not knowing better, we did the following. In order not to have too great a bend in the lead pipe between the cockpit floor and the hull, we fastened down that floor plank through which the scupper pipe goes without regard to the spacing of the floor planks out from the centerline of the boat. As the floor planking later progressed out from the centerline, we found, as we expected, the space between the plank last nailed down and the scupper plank to be of a less-than-standard width. We then laid one plank of lesser width here.

Now, before the whole floor is planked, put the lead scupper pipe in place. Then put a 1/4-inch-thick piece of stock, with a $1\frac{1}{2}$ inch hole drilled in it, over the pipe, and set this 1/4-inch spacing piece on the cockpit floor. With this as a guide, cut the pipe off flush. Remove the spacing piece. This makes the top of the pipe parallel to the floor with 1/4 inch left to hammer over into the rabbet. Of course, someone must hold the pipe securely at the other end (see fig. 36). Using the 1/4-inch spacer, saw off the other end of the pipe and hammer it firmly into its rabbet.

The bent-over ends are not fastened into the rabbet; thus there is no stress on the bent-over edge where the lead will otherwise certainly fail because of stress from the working of the hull. Check the scupper pipe for tightness each spring and, if required, swedge it firmly into its hole with a round, tapered bit of wood. Be sure to equip the scuppers with tapered softwood plugs to keep the water from backing up through the scuppers into the cockpit when heeled over.

Cockpit floor

The cockpit floor is laid from the centerline out. It lies tight to, and is bedded against, the bulkhead forward. It must go far enough out to the sides and aft to provide for a nailing piece for the cockpit staving. The cockpit floor is caulked to make a water-tight cockpit.

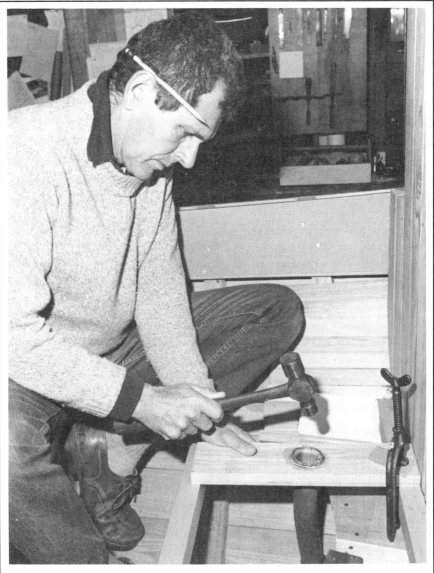

Fig. 36. Installing a cockpit scupper. *(Photo by Mary Anne Stets)*

Not knowing what the Crosbys did in an engineless boat, we put in access hatches on either side of the centerboard case and running a bit aft of it. These hatches are fastened down with screws and caulked. They are opened only seldom—once a year or so to check the ballast.

Deck Framing

The quarter knees should go in before the deck goes on and could well go in before the clamp. Generally the quarter knees in these boats are straight-grained. They notch around the last timberhead, and, as the deck lands on them, they must pitch up to the crown of the deck.

All deck frames (beams) must be notched into the clamp as described for the "main deck frame."

The crown of the deck was a problem for us; Bunk could only say, "we had a hundred deck frame patterns and they'd select them to do the particular job they wanted to do."

We knew what had to be done, however, and that is as follows. The deck frame at the forward end of the cabin trunk has a crown of 4-1/2 inches in 10 feet, as does all deck framing aft of this point. Forward of the cabin it is a bit more complex. In the profile view, the deck at the centerline of the boat is a straight line from the stem to the cabin trunk; thus, the mast partner and the king plank atop it are straight fore and aft.

Note well that the mast partner is 16 inches wide, and it must be no less, for consider this: the mast is 7-1/2 inches in diameter; the mast wedges are 3/4 to 7/8 inch; around all this the mast coat is fastened down by a 1/2-inch lead strip; there must be room on the oak king plank and mast partner for halyard and topping lift blocks on either side; and finally the mast step must be 3/4 to 1 inch wider than the king plank to provide a landing for the forward deck planking ends.

This all has bearing on the forward deck frames, for they must be flat on top where the width of the king plank (16 inches) bears upon them. It is this flat part of the deck frame that forms the straight line in profile from the stem to the cabin trunk. Lay these deck frames out accordingly.

Furthermore, the deck frames will each have a different camber. To help determine this, tack a string tight from the stem to the last full deck frame aft at the cabin trunk on the centerline of the boat. Now, from a straightedge square to the centerline and resting on the sheer strake (the clamp has to be notched to allow this), the heights from the sheer to the string may be measured for the intervening beams and used to calculate the crown of the beams.

Between the aftermost deck frame and the main deck frame at the bulkhead, the inboard ends of the half frames are supported temporarily by a 7/8-inch board sprung on top of the fore deck frames to the top of the aftermost deck frame. The ends of the half frames are temporarily clamped to this plank.

Now the "mast piece" can be put in. The Ralph Crosby plans show it notched into the forwardmost deck frame (see fig. 37), but Bunk Crosby said he did not do it this way.

At this point it is time to fair up the deck framing and the sheer as well.

Three or four men did this work on a twenty-foot catboat. It is all done by eye. The framing must be fair to receive the decking.

Forward Bulkhead

This forward bulkhead, like the after one, affords no structural strength; it is, rather, a bit of finish separating the cabin from the forward-most part of her (this unfinished area, where the ceiling is cut off and the mast is, can be used for stowage). The bulkhead is made up of the same staving as the cockpit and the after bulkhead of the cabin (see fig. 38).

Decking

Bunk Crosby felt very uneasy about the 7/8-inch decking we laid on our boat. He felt it should have been $1\frac{1}{8}$ inches square to give enough depth for "blind" fastenings and the caulking seam. There were some remnants of narrow deck planking on the Herbert Crosby catboat *Sarah*—it is 7/8 inch thick—and having only 7/8-inch cypress, we went with that. Bunk said that they always put down "narrow-laid" decks: "we always did that when I was there." Certainly this kind of deck, sprung to the outside curve of the hull, is very strong, much more so than a straight fore-and-aft-laid deck.

Fig. 37. The mast partner in place. *(Photo by Mary Anne Stets)*

fig. 38. The forward bulkhead in the cabin. Notice the finished transoms. *(Photo by Mary Anne Stets)*

First, the king plank must be put in, for the gunwale and planking butt against it. It is white oak and slightly less in width than the mast piece, thus allowing room for the deck ends to land on the mast piece (see fig. 39). There is also a short king plank aft between the cockpit staving and the transom. It has oak filler pieces fastened to its underside and projecting out from it to allow for the landing of after deck ends (see fig. 40).

Then the white oak gunwale, 3 inches wide and as thick as the decking, is steamed and bent in place on the boat. It butts against the king plank forward and the transom aft (see fig. 41). If, for lack of length in the gunwale stock, the gunwale must be more than one piece, the pieces are joined by a slash scarf; that is, a straight diagonal scarf about 12 inches long. This scarf is nailed horizontally through its edges from both the outside and the inside of the hull. These scarphs must have caulking seams.

The *Marshall*'s decking is 7/8-by-1$^{1}/_{8}$ inch cypress (pine was often used). The first deck plank is sprung in tight against the gunwale and then each additional strip of decking is sprung in place. The underside of each plank is beaded. The caulking seam is half the thickness of the plank (i.e., 3/8 inch). Butts land on the deck frames; they are caulked, and there must be two frame

Fig. 39. The kingplank lies atop the forward deck beams. The beams are let into the clamp and covered by the gunwale. *(Photo by Mary Anne Stets)*

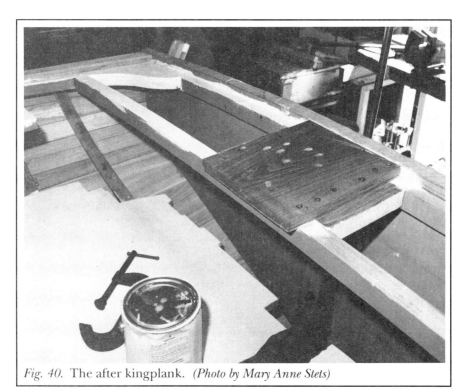

Fig. 40. The after kingplank. *(Photo by Mary Anne Stets)*

Fig. 41. Fitting the after end of the gunwale. *(Photo by Mary Anne Stets)*

bays between butts in adjacent planks. Each plank is toe-nailed into each deck frame, and between each deck frame three galvanized finish nails are blind-nailed through each plank into the plank it lays against. "Makes the best damn deck there is," said Bunk. The finish nails for blind-nailing are 2-inch nails set in no higher than the base of the caulking seam.

As each deck plank is nailed on, "witness" (mark) where each of the blind nails is on top of the plank so "you don't hit them when nailing in the next plank" (see fig. 42). When the deck is laid there are no fastenings showing.

Finishing The Deck

As the deck planking proceeds inwards toward the centerline of the boat, the curve of the cabin trunk and washboard must be taken into account. Most of the washboard and a bit of the trunk are parallel to the side of the boat; here they are an even number of planks in from the gunwale. As the curve of the washboard and trunk diverges from the side of the boat and begins to sweep in sharply towards the centerline, a guide is needed for cutting off the ends of the deck inside the boat. Picked up from the lofting, a pattern is made of the curve of the cabin trunk forward and another of the curve of the washboard aft.

Fig. 42. Caulking the deck. This caulking is rolled in, an easier and faster method when seams are uniformly tight. Notice the witness marks for the blind nails. *(Photo by Mary Anne Stets)*

Note that the deck ends two to three inches inside the cabin trunk, thus providing a shelf inside. When the deck is laid, using the pattern, draw a line for the outside of the cabin trunk, a line inside of this by 7/8 inch for the inside of the trunk, and a final line 2 to 3 inches inside of this for the end of the decking (see plans for the *Marshall*, plan 4).

Now the deck seams are caulked by rolling in a strand of cotton (see fig. 42). Then the deck is faired and smoothed by planing and sanding. In the 1920s the seams were paid with Khul's seam compound; it had to be heated first, but it was not tar or pitch. This being no longer available, we painted the deck seams after they were caulked and filled them with Pettit's seam compound, which contains a wax and presumably will keep the stuff elastic. After this it is time to give the deck its prime coat of paint.

Staving The Cockpit

The cockpit staving begins at the bulkhead port and starboard and meets at the centerline aft, where the last piece of staving is likely to be wider or narrower than the rest to fill the gap. At this time it is useful to have the rudder hung and a tiller or tiller pattern shipped to gauge the tiller slot in the staving. Install the staving with the slot already cut.

A nailing piece runs continuously along the cockpit floor plumb under the edge of the deck (see fig. 43). The lower ends of the staving are nailed to this, and to the deck itself, and to whatever else offers itself, such as the deck frame ends. These nails should be common nails, not finish nails. Of course the staving must come down tight on the cockpit floor. We bedded the staving ends; it seems that the Crosbys did not.

Cabin Trunk

With the deck laid and the cockpit staving in, preparations must be made to bend in the cabin trunk and the cockpit washboard. Using the template of the curve of the cabin trunk (previously used for finding the curve of the inside of the deck) redraw that line on the primed deck. Deduct 7/8 inch all around to get the line of the inside of the trunk. The trunk is fastened from the underside

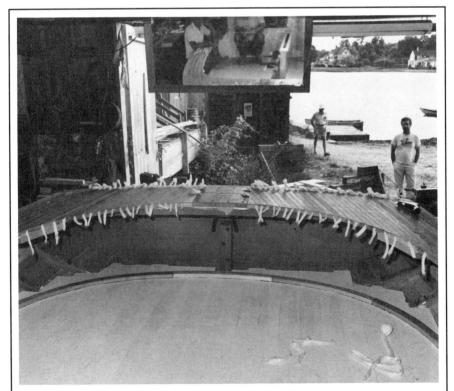

Fig. 43. The nailing strip for the cockpit staving aligns with the curved edge of the deck. *(Photo by Mary Anne Stets)*

Fig. 44. The juncture of the cabin trunk, cabin bulkhead, and washboard/ cockpit staving. *(Photo by Mary Anne Stets)*

of the deck up into the trunk. From the top of the deck down, between the lines for the inside and outside of the trunk, drill pilot holes for these fastenings every six inches or so. Deck seams and deck frames must be avoided.

Also at this time the "corner pieces" and the "head block" are installed. The corner pieces are the 2-by-4-inch white oak butt blocks to which the aft ends of the trunk are fastened. The top of each corner piece must pitch downwards towards the centerline to provide a landing for the aftermost trunk deck beam. The corner piece is fastened to the bulkhead; fastened, that is, from the bulkhead into the corner piece (see fig. 44).

The white oak head block, $1\,^1/_2$ inches thick, 6 inches high, and 11 inches long, securely anchors the forward ends of the two cabin trunk pieces. It is fastened up from the underside of the king plank, the forward face of the block being rounded to the curve of the cabin trunk. The top of the head block will receive the cabin trunk deck planks and should have enough extra wood on top to allow it to be cut to the camber and forward slope of that deck.

A bending form is now erected on the boat, around which to bend the cabin trunk. This consists of posts (we used 2-by-4s) standing vertically along the line representing the inside of the cabin trunk (previously drawn on the deck) and fastened to the shop ceiling. Where the trunk will be bent, the corners or edges of these posts should be rounded off. We screwed blocks of 2-by-4 stock to the lower sides of the posts and clamped these blocks firmly to the extra 2 to 3 inches of deck that extend inside of the trunk and provide the inside shelf. Perhaps the original and primary reason for the inside-the-trunk decking was to provide a landing place for the bending posts. The posts should be 8 to 10 inches apart where the bend is severest, 14 inches or so as the trunk runs aft (see fig. 45).

At this point we picked up trunk width (height) measurements from our lofting and marked these on the head block, bending posts, and cockpit staving. We tacked a batten to these marks, sighted it, adjusted it for fairness on one side, and then made the other side like the first.

The trunk is in two pieces, butted on the head block. These pieces are spiled for and gotten out of good white oak bending stock. Extra wood must be

Fig. 45. Bending posts for the cabin trunk. *(Photo by Mary Anne Stets)*

Fig. 46. The forward ends of the newly bent cabin trunk sides are clamped to the head block. *(Photo by Mary Anne Stets)*

left on top for fitting the trunk to the deck and also for the crown on top of the trunk deck. The top of the trunk is cut later. A few extra inches of length are left aft for fitting the butt there. Cut the forward butt end now; it must have a caulking bevel.

The two trunk pieces are steamed and put on the boat (one after the other), jacking them to the head block and then the posts as they are bent around (see fig. 46). Let them rest a day or so to take a set.

Now the trunk is fitted exactly to the deck. The Crosbys did this by scribing a line on the trunk parallel to the deck and as close to the deck as possible. This is done on the outside and the inside of the deck; the scribed line being at the same height from the deck on both sides. The trunk sides are then taken to the bench where they are planed precisely to these lines; they then fit the deck perfectly when put back on the boat. This procedure gets the line of the deck on the trunk as well as its bevels (the difference between the inside and outside lines) in one operation.

Now the butt forward should be fitted. Aft, 3/8 inch of the trunk thickness butts against the forward end of the staving. The remaining 1/2 inch will butt against the washboard when that is installed (see figs. 44 and 47).

Pick up the heights of the trunk from the marks on the head block, posts, and bulkhead, measure these distances up from the bottom edge of the trunk, and lay in a line on the trunk through these marks using a batten. This is the top of the trunk. When cutting to this line, make sure ample wood is left for the cabin deck camber.

Fig. 47. Tapping in the washboard where it butts against the trunk. *(Photo by Mary Anne Stets)*

The trunk bottom was primed and bedded slightly (in Dolphinite). We could not definitely ascertain whether, in the Crosby shops, this trunk-to-deck joint was caulked, or laid down on a strand of cotton, or only painted and bedded as we did. Through the previously drilled pilot holes, the deck-to-trunk fastenings are bored for and put in. Lastly, the trunk is fastened to the corner pieces. When the cabin trunk is completely fastened, the deck is greatly strengthened.

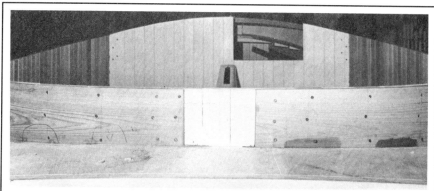

Fig. 48. The washboards are bent and screwed to the cockpit staving. *(Photo by Mary Anne Stets)*

Washboards

Although we had no specific instructions from Bunk on getting out the washboards (they are fairly easy to do), the following observations may be helpful. The top of the staving should be cut off before putting on the washboards. Note well that the top of the staving has an angle that must meet the camber of the cabin top, and this angle decreases and becomes square aft: it is a matter of fairing by eye.

The washboards are 1/2-inch-thick cypress and must be steamed. Where they butt against the trunk forward they must be caulked. Aft, they are notched into the washboard butt block. Because the washboard-butt block joints are covered by the cap rail, there is a little leeway in exactness for fitting here. The white oak washboard butt block aft is cut out to provide a pocket for the boom crotch. This pocket bottoms out above the deck and has two drain holes slanting down aft.

The washboards are fastened to every other cockpit stave (see fig. 48). This washboard-staving combination makes a very strong unity. The lower edge of the washboard goes from an over-bevel forward to an under-bevel aft. This should be a good fit and lightly bedded; otherwise it is a perfect water trap.

Finishing the Cabin Interior

Now, before the "top" is put on, it is time to finish the cabin interior, including the cupboards, finish painting work, and shelf edge (see fig. 49). This is standard boat carpentry.

Decking the Cabin

The cabin deck beams are dovetailed into the trunk (figs. 50 and 51). The cabin trunk deck of 3/4-by-3-1/4-inch tonge-and-groove cypress is laid and then canvased. This deck must be faired, primed with flat paint, and covered with a thickened white lead paint. Then the canvas is stretched and tacked down. The canvas is primed with a thin coat and finished with one or two color coats as required.

Fig. 49. The cabin cupboard and shelf. *(Photo by Mary Anne Stets)*

Fig. 50. The cabin trunk deck beam dovetails. *(Photo by Mary Anne Stets)*

Fig. 51. Installing the cambered cabin trunk deck beams. *(Photo by Mary Anne Stets)*

Finishing the Boat

Most of the remaining tasks are straightforward boat work: joining and caulking the hull, getting out the companionway and hatch, and putting on the trim. A few Crosby practices should be noted, however.

Ballasting the Centerboard

The centerboard is ballasted by cutting several 2-1/2-to-3-inch holes halfway or slightly more into the board with a hole saw, cleaning out the wood within the hole. Now the trick is simply to back cut (dovetail) each hole so that it is wider at the bottom than at the top. Thus, when lead is poured into the hole it is trapped in place.

Scribing the Waterline

This is a lovely method, particularly for a big boat in a small place, and also for its utter simplicity. The boat must be leveled athwartships. Erect a horizontal straightedge at the waterline at the bow and another at the stern; these must be at least a few inches wider than the boat is, level athwartships, and roughly perpendicular to the boat's centerline.

Stretch a chalk line between and over the two straightedges and tie a weight (for example, a lead duck) to each end of the line to keep it taut without sagging. This way the line can be slipped across the straightedges towards or away from the boat with the line always taut. Move the line in to touch the hull at her widest point and there tap in a small nail to mark the point. Slip the line over this nail and move the line in again so that it touches the boat forward of this and set in another nail with the line on top of this. Do this every six inches or so (depending on the shape of the boat) until reaching the stem. Do the same going aft and on the other side of the boat. Then, to mark in the waterline, take a batten about 6 feet long, 1 inch by 1/2 inch, and bend this against the hull, touching the nails. With this batten as a guide, scribe the waterline. A lumberman's scribe was commonly used for this.

Beeswax and Rosin

To cover up the heads of the fastenings we used the Crosby beeswax and rosin mixture. In fact, we used it as putty in other places as well, as long as there was no shrinking or swelling involved or a need for watertightness. Beeswax comes from wherever people take honey from bees, and rosin can be had from a good hardware store. Malcolm Crosby, Bunk's brother, said of this putty: "It would stay in place forever unless of course you come to burn the paint off a boat, of course you would melt it out." (Captain Malcolm Crosby/John Leavens interview, 1963.)

The beeswax-rosin putty has several advantages apart from being nontoxic and smelling good: after it hardens up, a little heat will render it supple and useful again even if it is a hundred years old, when joining the hull it provides a lubricant to make the joining easier, and it cuts like cheese.

Bunk said the Crosby mixture was about half and half by volume. These were the proportions we used, though mixed by eye, and with a little more rosin, as he later advised us. A heavy cast iron skillet is needed to melt down the wax over a hot plate. The wax and rosin mix when the wax has the consistency of peanut butter. It is applied directly to the boat from the frying pan, using a putty knife. It must be kept warm by trips back to the hot plate, and with a little bit of practice a rhythm is developed and the work goes quickly.

Fig. 52. Launching the *Breck Marshall. (Courtesy Tim Koverman Studio)*

A Closing Note
to Prospective Builders

Having replicated this boat, carefully considering how these boats were built, the size of the scantlings, the type of timber, and the shape of the boat itself, it is the conviction of the Seaport's boatbuilders that, taking into account economics and the boat's purposes, her construction cannot well be improved. At first we thought that her timbers were enormous, until we discovered that they were dubbed a bit for the planking, and until we considered the length of those timbers amidships. Furthermore, this 20-foot catboat has hardly any more structural strengthening attributes than an open boat, and a 20-foot by 10-foot open boat is quite a large one. As her clamp (perfectly tapered for its function) is not tied into her quarter knees or breasthook, her gunwale and planking carry that structural function, and it would be a great mistake to change her cypress planking for a lighter and weaker cedar hull or a needlessly heavier mahogany or hard pine one.

This wooden sailboat came at the bitter end of an evolutionary line, the end of a time when men in the boatyard, plus a blacksmith, knew how to fashion all of the materials that went into her making. To change this boat's construction, under the supposition that we, at the end of the twentieth century, know better, would be a presumptive error.

Fig. 53. (Photo by Mary Anne Stets)

Appendices

Appendix I

Tryphaena: the Background

Townsend Hornor of Osterville, Massachusetts, kindly ran down the following background on the catboat *Tryphaena*, whose lines were used to build the Seaport's *Breck Marshall*. *Tryphaena*, ex-*Towhee*, ex-*Active*, ex-*Mary*, ex-*Sally*, is a 20-foot catboat said to have been built about 1900 by Charles Crosby. She is credited to Herbert Crosby in *The Catboat Book*, but Wilton Crosby, Jr., suggests that she was built by Charles Crosby, since Herbert was active somewhat later. She was built as an unpowered work boat.

The earliest clear record of this boat dates to about 1952, when Robert Douglas of Vineyard Haven purchased the boat from Cyrus Sears, a carpenter in Vineyard Haven. At some earlier time she is said to have been owned by Manuel deFrates (or D. Frates) of Edgartown, who used her for scalloping. When Douglas bought her she had a 4-cylinder Lathrop engine that took up a lot of cabin space, so he installed a 1-cylinder Universal Fisherman.

Edwin Athearn, a marine broker from Centerville, Cape Cod, purchased her for $400 in the spring of 1955 from Robert Douglas and renamed her *Active*.

Carl Wolsieffer of Osterville purchased her for $450 in August 1955 from Athearn. He put in about twenty new frames, a new cockpit floor, companion-way frame, slide, etc. Wolsieffer installed a 1939 4-cylinder SeaScout engine and in 1956 renamed the boat *Towhee*.

She is currently owned by Jean Crosby, widow of Edward M. Crosby, who bought her from Carl Wolsieffer about 1975. In 1976-78 she was extensively rebuilt at the C.A. Crosby & Sons yard in Osterville. She received a new keel, centerboard box, centerboard, forefoot, mast step, many frames, 75 to 80 percent of the bottom planking, engine beds, transom, decks, cabin interior, rudder, and spars. A 4-cylinder Gray marine engine with 2:1 gear was installed. She was rigged in the summer of 1979. The cabin trunk and top had been rebuilt previously in plywood, and it was intended to replace them the following year. Renamed *Tryphaena*, a feminine proper name from the Bible, meaning delicate or luxurious, she is still sailed every summer by the Jean Crosby family. She is painted in the Pete Culler style.

Appendix II:

Specifications to Build a Crosby Catboat

This 1897 specification for the building of the 22-foot Herbert F. Crosby catboat *Goldenrod* is interesting for what it has to say about the materials used, the simplicity of contractual arrangements of that time, and the cost of obtaining such a boat. The $450 price of the boat, however, is only meaningful when set against the average annual wage in the United States at that time. It was $462! (*Catboat Association Bulletin* 51, November 1976)

SPECIFICATIONS.

Length Over All	22 ft	Draught	24 in
Length Water Line		Square or ~~Overhang~~ Stern	
Length Keel		Length Cockpit	12 ft
Extreme Beam	20 " 6in	Length Cabin	9 ft in
	19 " in		

DIMENSIONS OF SPARS. **DIMENSIONS OF SAIL.**

Mast		Foot	29 ft
Boom		Hoist	1 ft
Gaff		Head	19 "
		Leech	

FITTINGS. **KINDS OF STOCK.**

Blocks	Wood or Composition	Keel	Oak
~~Pat. Hoist~~		Timbers	"
Hoops	"	Plank	Cypress
Rigging	manila	Deck	Pine
Traveler		Cockpit Floor	Pine Wood tight
Stem Piece	Composition	Cockpit Sheathing	Cypress
Oars		Cockpit Seat	
Anchors	one each	Cabin Slide	
Roads		~~Cabin Doors~~	on one side
Ventilators		Cabin Trunk	Oak round end
Steerer		Cabin Ceiling	
Wheel		Cabin Closets	
Tiller	"	Cabin Tables	Cypress
Ballast	Stone	Cabin Shelves	
Stay	Wire	Fastening	Copper galvanized

PAINT AND VARNISH.

Outside	White	Cockpit	Paint
Bottom	Copper	Cabin	Varnish
Deck	Paint	Spars	"
Cabin Top	canvas Painted		

EXTRAS.

With Boom Well Price $450.
Hard pine sheathing on keel 1¼ in thick

Herbert F. Crosby

I hereby agree to the foregoing.
Everett A. Boole

-60-

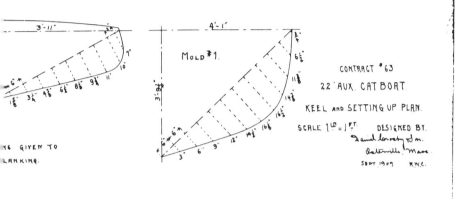

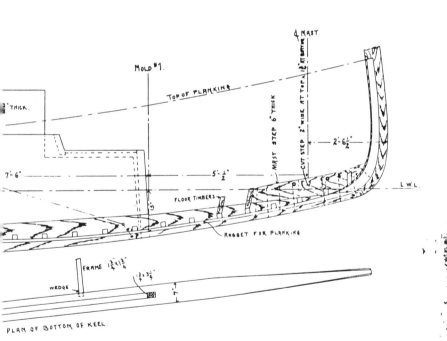

Plan 1 *(Courtesy Crosby Yacht Yard, Inc.)*

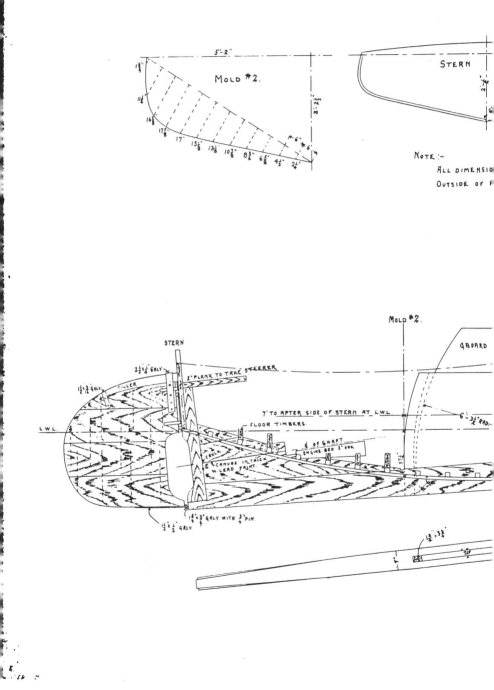

MOLD #2.

5'-2"

STERN

2'-2½"

NOTE :–
ALL DIMENSIO
OUTSIDE OF P

STERN

QBOARD

MOLD #2.

1" PLANK TO TAKE STEERER

7' TO AFTER SIDE OF STERN AT L.W.L.

FLOOR TIMBERS.

6 - 3¼" RAD.

£ OF SHAFT
ENGINE BED 5" OAK

2¼×¾ GALV.
1½×¾ GALV.
TILLER

CAULK
CANVAS 1" THICK
IN LEAD PAINT.

L.W.L.

1¾×¾ GALV.
1¼×¾×3" GALV. WITH ¾" PIN.

MYSTIC SEAPORT MUSEUM INC.
MYSTIC CONNECTICUT
CAPE COD CATBOAT "BRECK MARSHALL"
LINES & OFFSETS
DRAWN BY C. POSTON   DATE MARCH 15, 1987
SCALE 1¾" = 1 FOOT   SHEET 1 OF 6
ACCESSION NO 86.10

MASS. 10 NOV 1985 FROM THE CATBOAT TRYPHAENA
RE LOA-20', LWL-19'9', BEAM-9'8', DRAFT-2'3.

Plan 2

OFFSETS · FEET · INCHES · EIGHTHS TO OUTSIDE OF PLANKING

| STATION | HALF BREADTHS | | | | | | | | | | HEIGHTS | | | | | |
	SHEER	WL48"	WL42"	WL36"	LWL	WL24"	RABBET	DIAG A	DIAG B	DIAG C	SHEER	BUT1'	BUT2'	BUT3'	RABBET	KEEL
TRANS.	3-4-5	3-5-1	3-2-6	1-11-7	0-7-3	—	0-1-2	3-11-2	3-10-0	3-7-5	4-3-7	2-8-1	3-0-0	3-4-1	2-4-6	0-4-0
1	3-9-4	3-9-6	3-8-7	3-1-7	1-10-2*	0-2-0	0-1-4	4-4-2	4-3-1	4-0-5	4-2-2	2-3-2	2-7-2	2-11-2	1-11-7	0-4-4
2	4-4-4	4-4-4	4-4-3	4-2-0	3-8-2	2-0-6	0-2-3	4-11-6	4-11-1	4-8-6	4-0-2	1-7-7	1-11-6	2-3-5	1-4-7	0-6-1
3	4-9-5	4-9-4*	4-9-4*	4-8-2	4-4-6	3-4-7	0-3-3	5-5-1	5-4-3	5-2-1	3-11-5	1-3-3	1-6-7	1-10-3	1-0-7	0-8-3
4	4-8-7	4-9-0	4-9-1	4-7-6	4-4-2	3-5-2	0-3-4	5-4-6	5-4-1	5-2-1	4-0-6	1-3-1	1-6-3	1-10-1	1-1-0	0-10-1
5	4-3-2	4-3-2	4-2-5	4-0-4	3-8-2	2-8-1	0-3-4	4-10-1	4-10-4	4-9-6	4-3-3	1-5-2	1-9-1	2-1-5	1-2-4	1-0-0
6	3-4-4	3-3-7	3-2-4	2-11-2	2-6-2	1-6-3	0-3-0	3-10-1	3-11-4	4-0-3	4-7-6*	1-9-7*	2-2-5	3-0-7	1-4-2	1-2-1
7	2-2-0	2-0-5	1-10-5	1-7-2	1-3-1*	0-7-6	0-2-2	2-6-0	2-7-5	2-9-2	5-1-1	2-3-5*	3-9-5	—	1-7-2	1-5-2
8	1-1-5*	1-0-3	0-10-6	0-8-5	0-6-3*	0-2-7	0-1-7	1-4-2	1-5-3	1-6-6	5-5-1	5-10-2	—	—	1-10-3	1-9-3
STEM	0-1-4	0-1-4	0-1-4	0-1-4	0-1-4	0-1-4	0-1-4	0-1-5	0-1-7	0-2-0	5-8-5	—	—	—	—	—

DIAGONAL-A IS (5-8-5) UP ℄ FROM BASELINE : (5-1-5) OUT LWL FROM ℄.
DIAGONAL-B IS (5-8-5) UP ℄ FROM BASELINE : (4-8-5) OUT WL 24" FROM ℄.
DIAGONAL-C IS (5-8-5) UP ℄ FROM BASELINE : (3-10-3) OUT WL 24" FROM ℄.

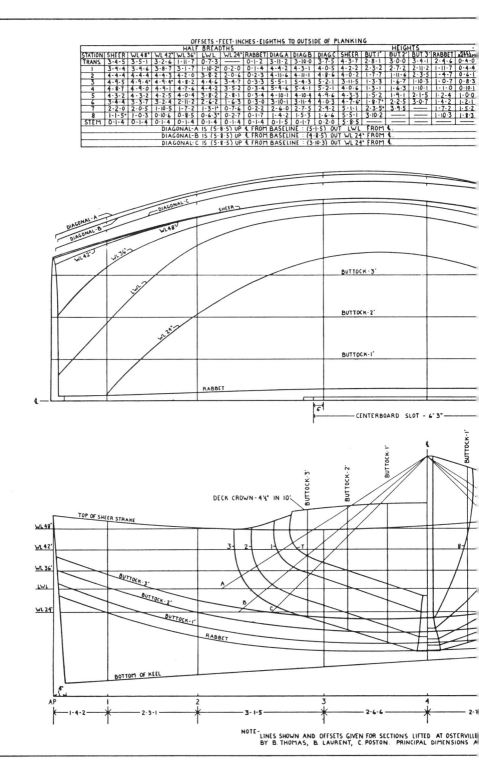

CENTERBOARD SLOT - 6' 3"

DECK CROWN - 4¼" IN 10'

NOTE- LINES SHOWN AND OFFSETS GIVEN FOR SECTIONS LIFTED AT OSTERVILLE
BY B. THOMAS, B. LAURENT, C. POSTON. PRINCIPAL DIMENSIONS A

- SHELF EDGE - CYPRESS - ½" × 3".
- HEAD BLOCK - W. OAK - 1½" × 6" × 11" - TO TAKE FWD. JOINT IN TRUNK - FASTENED TO KING PLANK.
- CORNER PIECE - W. OAK - 2" × 4" - TO TAKE AFT. END OF TRUNK AT BULKHEAD - NOTE ALSO SHOWN SHEET 6.
- TRUNK - W. OAK - ⅞" - STEAM BENT - NOTCHED TO TAKE TRUNK DECK BEAMS.
- COCKPIT STAVING - CYPRESS - ¾" × 3½" TONGUE & GROOVE - NOTE SLOT FOR TILLER CLEARANCE.
- WASHBOARD - CYPRESS - ½" STEAM BENT AROUND STAVING.
- BUTT BLOCK - W. OAK - 2½" × 6½" × 13" - NOTCHED TO TAKE BOOMCROTCH.
- CAP - W. OAK - ⅞" × 2½" - NOTE MUST FAIR IN WITH HALF ROUND ON TRUNK.
- SEAT STANTION - W. OAK - 2" × 2" - TURNED - REMOVABLE.
- CLEAT - CYPRESS - ½" × ⅞" - FASTENED TO COCKPIT FLOOR.
- COCKPIT SEAT - CYPRESS - ⅞" - REMOVABLE.
- CLEAT - W. OAK - 14" - TO TAKE SHEET.
- TRUNK DECK BEAMS - W. OAK - 1¼" × 1¾" - HALVED INTO TRUNK WITH HALF-DOVETAIL - CROWN - 7" IN 7'-8".
- DOOR SILL - W. OAK - 1" × 3½".
- DOOR POST - W. OAK - 1⅜" × 3¼" - NOTCHED TO LAND TRUNK DECK - GROOVED TO TAKE ¾" HATCH BOARDS.
- TRUNK DECK - CYPRESS - ¾" × 3¼" TONGUE & GROOVE - CANVAS COVERED.
- HEADER - W. OAK - 1⅞" × 2¾".
- SLIDE PIECE - W. OAK - 1⅜" - GROOVED TO TAKE SLIDE.
- FINISH - CYPRESS - ½" × 2".
- SLIDE - TRUNK DECK STOCK.
- SLIDE FRAME - W. OAK - 1¼" SQUARE.
- HALF ROUND - W. OAK - ½" × ⅞".
- MOULDING - CYPRESS - ½" × 1½" - NOTE SECTIONAL VIEW SHOWN ON SHEET 6.
- FIXED LIGHT - 10½" × 3" - PORT & STBD.
- DECK RIBBAND - W. OAK - ⅞" × 1½" - NOTE LIMBER HOLES - ⅜" × 1½" - 2 OR 3 PORT & STBD.
- HALF ROUND - W. OAK - ⅞" × 1⅝".
- RUDDER - W. OAK - 1½".
- GUDGEONS & PINTLES - BRONZE CASTINGS.
- TILLER STRAPS - ¼" × 1½" FLAT STOCK.
- TILLER - W. OAK - 2½" × 3½" AT TRANSOM - TAPERS TO 1½" EITHER END.
- CENTERBOARD - W. OAK - 1⅜" - PIN IS 1" DIA. - NOTE LEAD POCKETS SHOWN ON SHEET 2.
- TRAVELER - ¾" ROD STOCK - TO TAKE SHEET BLOCK.
- QUARTER CLEATS - W. OAK - 11" - PORT & STBD.
- CLEATS ON BULKHEAD - W. OAK - 8" - THREE ON PORT SIDE TO TAKE HALYARDS AND LIFT.
- MOORING CLEAT - W. OAK - 11".
- TURNING BLOCKS - BRONZE - SINGLE TO STBD. - DOUBLE TO PORT - TO TAKE HALYARDS AND LIFT.
- STEM BAND - BRONZE - ¾" HALF ROUND.
- SHACKLE - ½" DIA. STOCK - TO TAKE STAY.
- MOORING CHOCK - PORT & STBD.
- MAST WEDGES - CYPRESS.
- CLEAT - W. OAK - 7¼" - TO TAKE C.B. PENNANT - NOTE PIN THRU C.B. AT TOP OF BOX.

CONSTRUCTION DETAILS TAKEN FROM THE CAPE COD CATBOAT SARAH BUILT BY HERBERT
F. CROSBY, DRAWINGS BY DANIEL CROSBY & SONS OF CONTRACTS #14, #62, AND #63, AND
INTERVIEWS WITH MR. H. MANLEY CROSBY JR. AT OSTERVILLE, MASS.

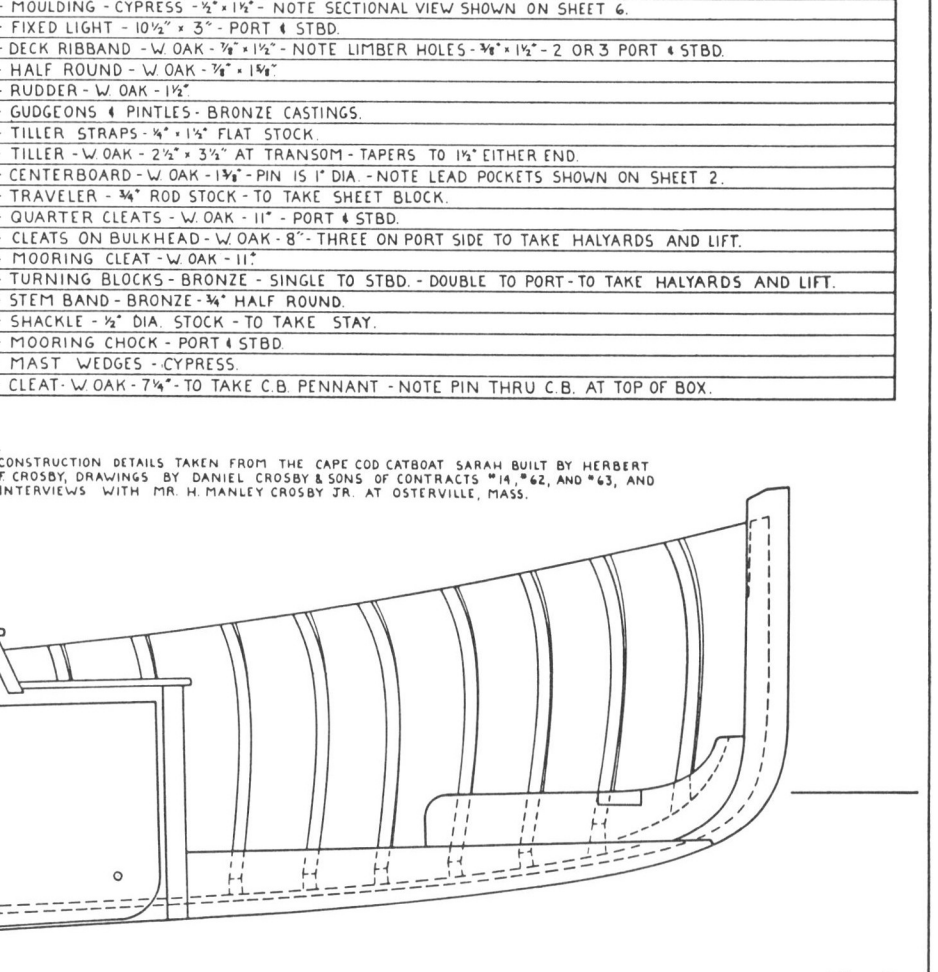

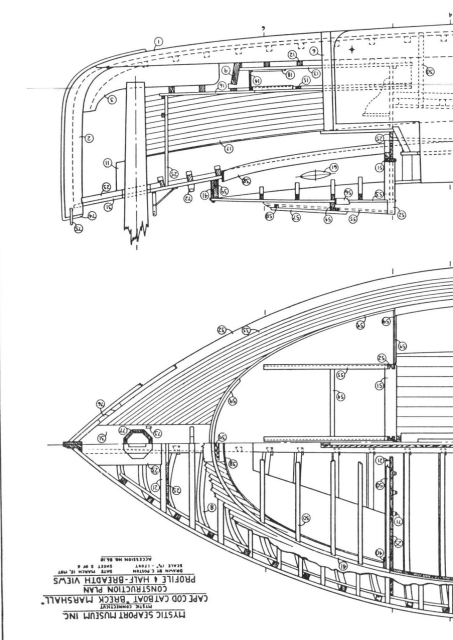

SECTION THRU BULKHEAD
(LOOKING FWD)

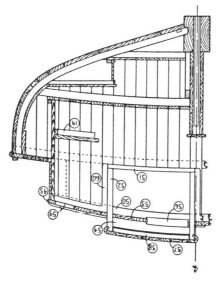

FEET AND INCHES

0 1 2 3 4

MYSTIC SEAPORT MUSEUM INC.
MYSTIC CONNECTICUT
CAPE COD CATBOAT "BRECK MARSHALL"
CONSTRUCTION PLAN
SECTIONAL VIEWS
DRAWN BY C POSTON   DATE MARCH 15, 1987
SCALE 1½" = 1 FOOT   SHEET 4 OF 6
ACCESSION NO 86.10

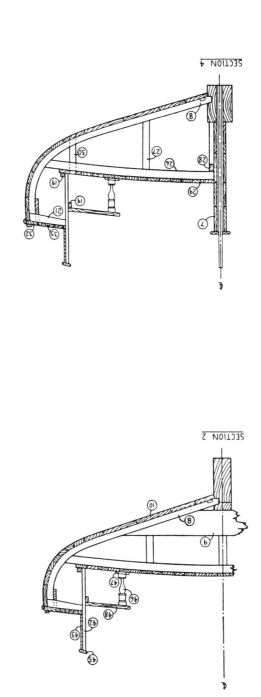

SECTION 4

SECTION 2

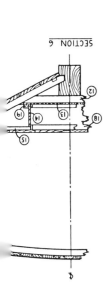

SECTION 6

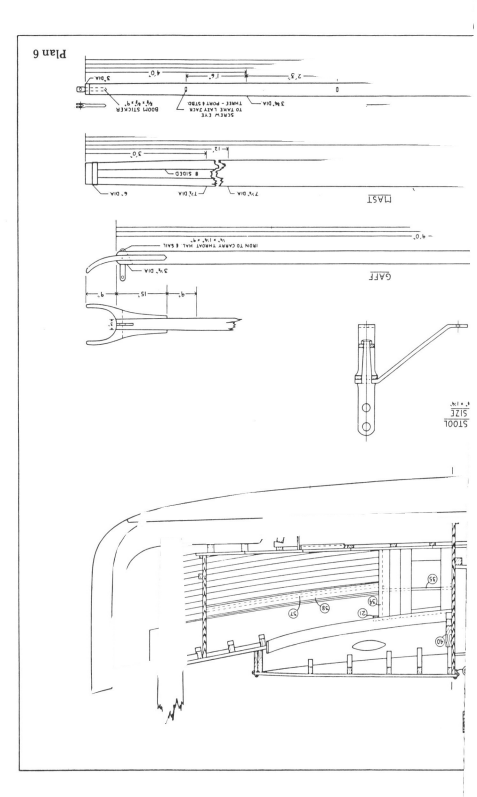

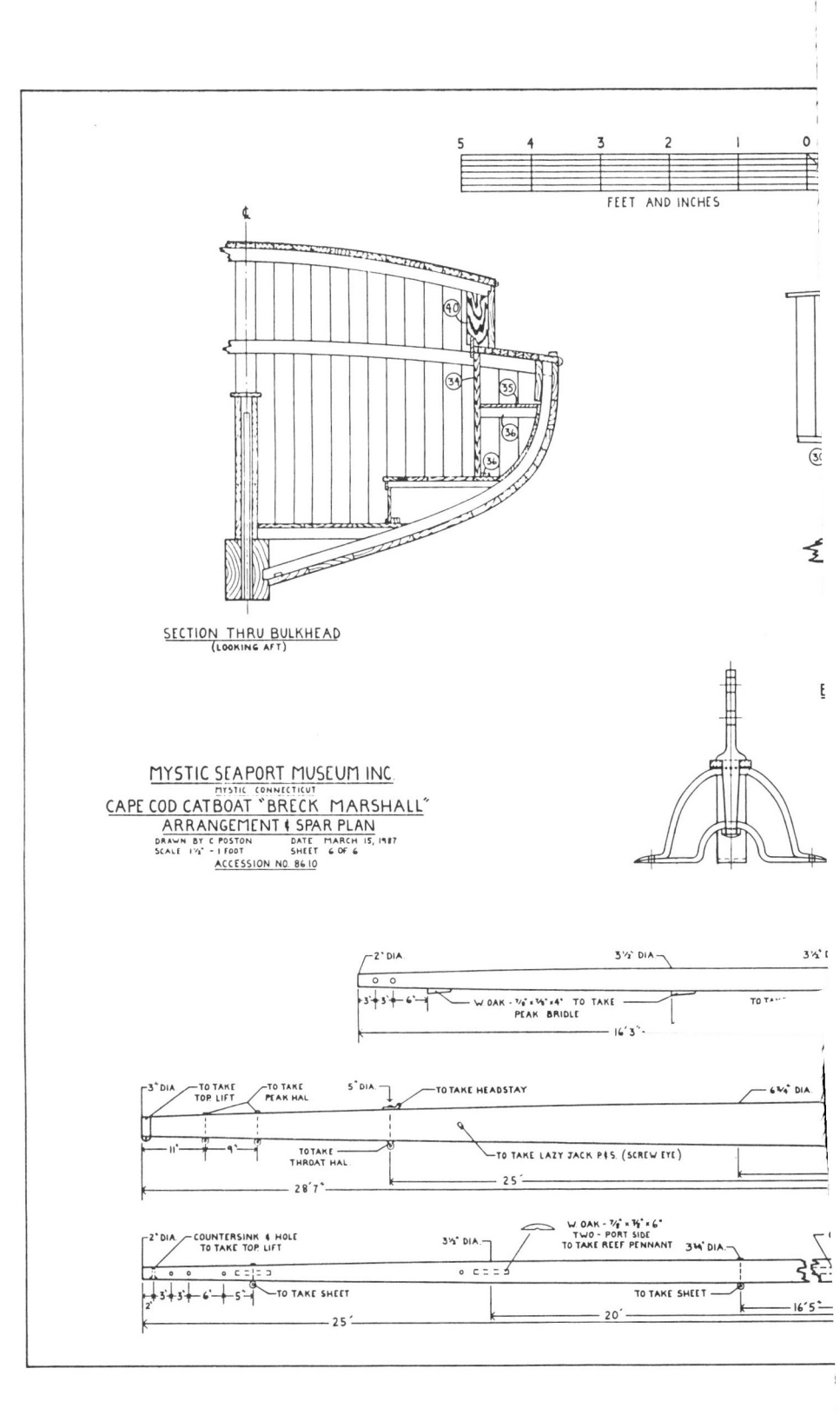

5 4 3 2 1 0

FEET AND INCHES

SECTION THRU BULKHEAD
(LOOKING AFT)

MYSTIC SEAPORT MUSEUM INC.
MYSTIC CONNECTICUT
CAPE COD CATBOAT "BRECK MARSHALL"
ARRANGEMENT & SPAR PLAN

DRAWN BY C POSTON   DATE MARCH 15, 1987
SCALE 1½" = 1 FOOT   SHEET 6 OF 6
ACCESSION NO. 86.10

2" DIA   3½" DIA   3½"
W OAK - ⅞" × ⅝" × 4" TO TAKE
PEAK BRIDLE
3" + 3" + 6"
16' 3"

3" DIA — TO TAKE   — TO TAKE   5" DIA   — TO TAKE HEADSTAY   6¾" DIA
TOP LIFT   PEAK HAL.
TO TAKE
THROAT HAL.   TO TAKE LAZY JACK P & S. (SCREW EYE)
11"   9"
28' 7"   25'

2" DIA — COUNTERSINK & HOLE   3½" DIA   W OAK - ⅞" × ⅝" × 6"   3¼" DIA
TO TAKE TOP LIFT   TWO - PORT SIDE
TO TAKE REEF PENNANT
3" + 3" + 6" + 5"   — TO TAKE SHEET   o c ===3   TO TAKE SHEET   16' 5"
2"
25'   20'

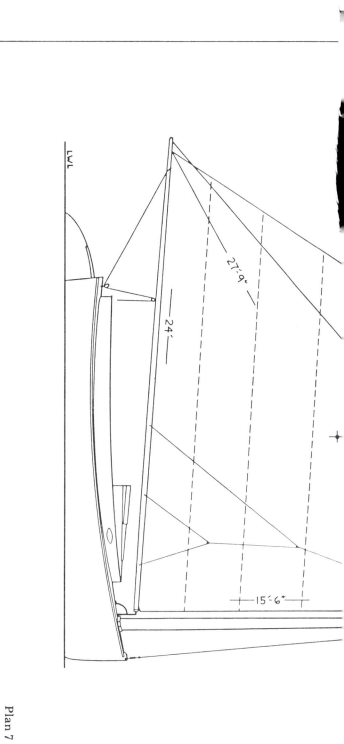

LWL

27'·9"

24'

15'·6"

MYSTIC SEAPORT MUSEUM INC.
MYSTIC CONNECTICUT

CAPE COD CATBOAT "BRECK MARSHALL"

SAIL PLAN

DRAWN BY C POSTON
SCALE ⅛" – 1 FOOT

DATE MARCH 15, 1987
SHEET 5 OF 6

ACCESSION NO 8610

NOTE –
THIS SAIL PLAN TAKEN FROM CONTRACT ➤ 53,
DANIEL CROSBY & SON, OSTERVILLE, MASS 1907.